ROBERT DESNOS FINDS
HIS SLEEP MEDICINES
BENEATH BACHELARD'S
FLOORBOARDS

Also by George Kalamaras

Poetry Books

To Sleep in the Horse's Belly: My Greek Poets and the Aegean Inside Me (2023)
What My Hound Dog Is Scenting Through the Sloughgrass Is a Way of Scenting Me (2023)
Marsupial Mouth Movements (2021)
Through the Silk-Heavy Rains (2021)
We Slept the Animal: Letters from the American West (2021)
Luminous in the Owl's Rib (2019)
That Moment of Wept (2018)
The Hermit's Way of Being Human (2015)
Kingdom of Throat-Stuck Luck (2011)
The Recumbent Galaxy (2010)
  (with Alvaro Cardona-Hine)
Gold Carp Jack Fruit Mirrors (2008)
Even the Java Sparrows Call Your Hair (2004)
Borders My Bent Toward (2003)
The Theory and Function of Mangoes (2000)

Poetry Chapbooks

Bootsie in the Bardo (2023)
The Shoes of the Fisherman's Wife Are Some Jive-Ass Slippers (2021)
The Mining Camps of the Mouth (2012)
Symposium on the Body's Left Side (2011)
Your Own Ox-Head Mask as Proof (2010)
The Scathering Sound (2009)
Something Beautiful Is Always Wearing the Trees (2009)
  (with paintings by Alvaro Cardona-Hine)
Beneath the Breath (1988)
Heart Without End (1986)

Critical Study

Reclaiming the Tacit Dimension: Symbolic Form in the Rhetoric of Silence (1994)

ROBERT DESNOS FINDS HIS SLEEP MEDICINES BENEATH BACHELARD'S FLOORBOARDS

George Kalamaras

MadHat Press
Cheshire, Massachusetts

MadHat Press
MadHat Incorporated
PO Box 422, Cheshire, MA 01225

Copyright © 2024 George Kalamaras
All rights reserved

The Library of Congress has assigned
this edition a Control Number of
2024937878

ISBN 978-1-952335-81-5 (paperback)

Words by George Kalamaras
Author photo: George with Blaisie (as a puppy at approximately twelve weeks), by Mary Ann Cain
Cover image: Man Ray, *Robert Desnos in Andre Breton's Studio in 1922 (Desnos dans l'atelier de Breton)* © Man Ray 2015 Trust / Artists Rights Society (ARS), NY / ADAGP, Paris 2024
Cover design by Marc Vincenz

www.MadHat-Press.com

First Printing
Printed in the United States of America

for Mary Ann and Blaisie

*and for Judy Johnson,
who brought Bachelard into my life
thirty-five years ago*

*Grandeur progresses in the world in proportion
to the deepening of intimacy.*
—Gaston Bachelard

How simple and strange everything is.
—Robert Desnos

Table of Contents

Waiting for Your Echo to Enlarge Me

The Speaking Point	3
Dostoevsky's Donkey Ride	4
The Hole	5
The Archaeology of Light	6
We Might Somehow Save the Waning	8
Release the Dark Birds	10
Blur	11
Why I Kept Asking	12
Anna Akhmatova and the Broken Bones of Sleep	14
Jacques Cousteau Was a Splendid Blue Shadow	16
The Psychoanalysis of Fire	18
Centuries of My Any-Human-Pain	20
Waiting for Your Echo to Enlarge Me	21

Scraps of Said in the Infinite Dark

Unreliable Narrator	25
In the Time of Borges and Calm	26
Mizzle	28
Concessionary Recompense	30
My Vocabulary Did This to Me	31
Elongation of the In-Between	32
No One Persecuted a Single Word	34
Scraps of Said in the Infinite Dark	35
Now We Return to Sorrow	36
Separation of the Primal Pneuma	37
Simply by Breathing	38
Bachelard Finds Himself Beneath His Own Floorboards and Realizes the Rain in His Gut Is an Epiphany	39
I Beg Robert Desnos to Heal Me	40

Every Word I Spoke

Bingo	45
The Long Ride	46
Black Threads of Gold	48
Anywhere We Step	50
Clockwork	51
Home	52
Every Word I Spoke	53
Traveling North	54
This, Our Family	55
We Knew Something Good	56
The Fifth Manifesto	57
It Takes More Than a Million Lives Just to Become Human	58
Aspects of the Almost-Arriving Moon	60

The Meticulous Mice of the Lantern-Lathed Tongue

After Thirty-Two Years	65
What Makes the Repetitions in Our Head Is Only an Interruption in the Death Dream of Robert Desnos	66
There Seemed Nowhere Else to Go	68
Brahms by Firelight	69
I Would Tongue of It and Plead	70
The Meticulous Mice of the Lantern-Lathed Tongue	72
Fire-Eater	74
A Brief History of Mirrors	75
Yes, Our Internal Organs Knew Better	76
Jacques Cousteau and the Dark Lengths of Rain	78
Kurosawa Sometimes Wept Inside Kawabata's Dream	80
Photo of Brahms on His Deathbed	82
Robert Desnos Finds His Sleep Medicines Beneath Bachelard's Floorboards	84

Borges and the Library of Babel

Michael Mitsakis Thought That Every Six Was a Nine	89
Zorba the Greek	90

At the Corner of Vallejo and Wang Wei	92
Borges and the Library of Babel	94
A Quarter of an Hour to Search Within	96
Every Word I Failed to Read	97
House Hunting During the Egg-Laying Season of Moths	98
This Is How We Know Poetry Matters	100
This Skin or That	102
We Remember the Subject of Love	103
Recalcitrant Owl on Fire in the Humble Boy's Chest	104
I Could Not Quite Speak	105
House and Universe	106
Notes	109
Acknowledgments	111
About the Author	113

Waiting for Your Echo to Enlarge Me

The Speaking Point

Here is where I find the speaking point.
1900–1945. *Dream Renderer. Poet. Oak Tree Whose Leaves Are on Fire with Fierce Unrequited Love.*

In each successive heaven, an eyebrow like a cloud-packed volcano.
Eruption of solid hair crowds my sight so that I am here. Now.

Mark the start of one of the most daring literary adventures of the sleep gate.
Ask yourself north so that you might sense the sparrow distance between tough and tongue. Tender and torn.

A long time from now, I might be alive.
When one of many Buddhas returned, we knew the body as a transient gag.

I have stepped into a word as I have stepped into this life.
One body at a time, with a basket of eggs, we count the balance of death and girth. Seek stability in the way definitions define.

One of the most. He is the author of. She and she have each published a farm disguised as a book.
Robert Desnos. René Daumal. Simone Kahn and Suzanne Césaire.

George: farmer, tiller of the earth.
I pull the flowers. I tend the weeds.

George Kalamaras

Dostoevsky's Donkey Ride

So it came to pass that every day I wore three shoes.
I wore two on my feet and a third around my neck like a
	medallion.

You might say I was an angry weather pattern.
You might place garlic in the mouths of the dead, even now
	during the seeping of starlight.

Say the entire footprint of the fallen garage was enough to
	house the wind.
Say there are copycat heartbeats pounding in our chests.

Siberia, back in 1849, was one of the coldest places on earth.
Most of its fur-bearing foxes knew enough to den-up, away
	from comeliness and greed.

Once, I rode a burro through the streets of Juárez.
My sombrero bore the mark of the moon like a heavy stone
	soughing goodnight.

My Cleopatra headdress said that in a former life I'd been a
	milk snake of a man without the woman part of my heart.
When Geronimo surrendered, and the Chiricahuas got the
	coughing sickness, their train ride into exile in Florida was
	a death rattle caught in the throat many years in the long
	way down.

The Hole

At that time, the ants of Fiji were nearly unknown to me and
 my fellow entomologists.
In the evening, dinner was served by barelegged rooster men.

From the initials of your name, I could detect you thought me
 left-handed.
Nearby, a Hindu festival for some enormous tree was
 underway, but they garlanded *me*, blessing me with holy
 water. My arm steady and posed as a branch.

Still, red clay territory might say more about an infestation of
 ironwood and pandanus palms.
It might guide my whiskey breath back toward what the British
 referred to benignly as, *Carve the Queen's name into your
 heart.*

At that time, time was not an issue; every tissue of our bodies
 swirled.
I recalled Lambasa, as if it were three days from now, and
 spread jam on thick slices of taro.

The social promotion of the letters of my name had
 astounded me, even elevating the city of Suva to a status
 that required reading competence of my ant-self ways.
Mound upon mound of past lives gathered around me, bitten
 and stung, until I recognized the decomposed underbelly
 of a beetle our group had killed and carried triumphantly
 to the hole.

George Kalamaras

The Archaeology of Light

Then it was as if a rainstorm in the belly.
As if one of us had swallowed an entire deck of cards.

My childhood was fiercing about inside me.
There were sharks in the watery depths. Instead of the color
    gray, the archipelago was broken into bodies of insolent bats.

Prawns and fish consisted of a higher life.
There was a considerably long adaptation of seasonal change
    reminding us that all things must pass.

Yes, the Hindu scriptures had said as much, but is reaching
    the reddish dorsal fin of the throat an act of kerosene or
    allegiance?
Can we ever step fully from the storm-ridden word, struggling
    the tongue, making it too tough to speak among all the
    dimming lamps?

I had been commissioned to dig for bones wherever I could.
I discovered that the audital bullae of the skull of the musk
    deer can, indeed, become enlarged beyond expectation.

East of the Altai Mountains and south of the Yablonoi there
    is a landlocked 4,000-foot plateau that extends into the
    Gobi and nearly down into the Ordos.
In Shantung Province, I encountered a remarkable river
    depositing silt somehow into the soft tissue of my brain.

Robert Desnos Finds His Sleep Medicines...

I buried my memories.
I buried some meat there and allowed the maggots to hatch therein.

George Kalamaras

We Might Somehow Save the Waning

I have said that there are two classes of dung beetles.
Fleas, ticks, and flies also lay their eggs in feces.

I have said that the last days of the wild Mongolian ass were
    fast approaching.
That if we resisted apricots, grapes, and great masses of sand,
    we might somehow save the waning.

There were lamas who sang in the temple halls of Linga Gompa.
And one who was immured in a cave at dawn.

Finally, great migrations of red-crowned cranes blessed me
    simply by flying over.
Intoxicants, long embedded in the flesh, reminded us of a river
    gone wrong.

The pleasant hours were spent throwing salt over the shoulder.
    Then into a wound. Then into the sea we knew was our
    mouth.
We pleaded for a linguist. A mapmaker. For *anyone* who could
    scup the tongue.

On second thought, perhaps there are three classes of dung
    beetles. Maybe four.
Some are *rollers*. Others, *tunnelers*. Still others are known as
    dwellers.

Robert Desnos Finds His Sleep Medicines...

Yes, like them, I am often attracted by the dung collected by a burrowing owl.
Sometimes I fly. Sometimes I dig. Sometimes, as I sink, I massage the gold dust of words right out of the ground.

George Kalamaras

Release the Dark Birds

I've cut open the dictionary again to release the dark birds.
I've opened the cage of my chest as if I were a Magritte
 painting.

Canebrake. Cocklebur. Swamp oak in my mouth.
More than my past is sinking.

There is always a river and always some expedition or other
 onto which I have signed.
I know of both the White and Blue Nile, but I have lost
 basketfuls of bread. Heirlooms and snails.

Take the river reeds and weave them into a hat.
Say *Mexican sombrero* three times with your head turned to
 the left.

Cough gently into the inguinal gap of words.
Bend over the medical table for the digitally probing poem.

Cut off pieces of yourself and place them randomly into the
 open book.
The dictionary can now be renamed *Book Without Birds* or
 The Book of Exasperated Collage.

Blur

It's true that a little eelgrass withstands the trembling of love
    bites.
I can already hear the fear of fascism in each melancholic note.

The cello concerto from 1936 is a hummingbird silvering
    open the moon.
The distant sound of three a.m. trains is a palpable pulse.

Listen how I make a thunderclap into a womb.
Attune yourself to the coal flames inside a tree.

Shoulder my love like a vibrating gillyflower.
Tremble touch the trebling willow and bend of it and bleed.

There is a passionate sea disguised as a mirage of stars.
Sometimes wind rises from the bottom of a condemned foot.

Below the hammered centuries there are fugitive rakes
    reflected in an echo of gravel notes.
I have made a mess of my life. I ask that you seek the blur of
    the spiritually soaked in the many candles asking the sand-
    grasp of my chest.

George Kalamaras

Why I Kept Asking

Tired from the desert heat, from rock face and scorpion, we
 returned to the lamasery at Kounbourn.
I had tried living a life of sensual pleasure. Each touch—each
 moment of tongue—only brought me despair.

Eating and drinking sure enough fill one's belly, but what hermit
 cave might we step into to satisfy what the earth craves?
Seems as if the unrained sky continuously lays its anvil down
 upon our shoulders as one way to urge us toward dissolve.

Those former lives in Kyoto skilled me in tea.
The art of poetry is one thing. Gastronomy another.

I still recall the gorgeous figures of the women who laid the
 tea tray before me.
Slender hands. Pale white skin glistening next to the sea-
 oat green of a cup of Gyokuro steeped in water heated
 precisely to 160 degrees.

When the caravan men arrived with questions about the inner
 light, it was the Mongolians who hunted with eagles to
 whom I directed them.
When they asked after the best fuel to heat their tents against
 cold desert nights, I showed them my pipe embers and a
 pile of simmering camel dung.

Someone asked me why I kept asking them things?
One traveler insisted that direction was a linguistic itch? An
 irreparable invention?

Robert Desnos Finds His Sleep Medicines...

We arrive like moonlight across the night-dark sand.
We come so many times into a body and out that we ask
 of the moon to guide us. To hide us with it inside the
 Bactrian humps of a camel moving from here to there.
 There to here. Here to everywhere at once.

George Kalamaras

Anna Akhmatova and the Broken Bones of Sleep

Part of the underwater underside is breaking apart.
I no longer understand a concept simple as linear time. Or
  even wind inside a windless rain.

Or is the irrefutable truly a mackle of estranged music?
I went to the astrologer and discovered a thirteenth sun sign,
  one hovering over the invisible fourteenth chakra the
  sadhu in Banaras had told me about so many summers ago
  on cremation grounds.

That was the year Anna Akhmatova and I fell in love.
The arc in her Romanesque nose was enough to stupefy me
  into something more than a crush.

What can I tell you about those winter months in St. Petersburg?
Not enough wood in the fire. A few beets in a bit of thin broth.
  Nourishment coming only in the form of fierce bouts of
  kissing.

I'm ashamed to say I cheated on her, having an affair with the
  famous ballerina Vera Karalli.
I'm not speaking in metaphors. Look at my diary. Each ant I
  crushed—whose sunburnt body I had recorded in those
  pages—was a penance for my misdeeds.

Anna knew about Vera but only after I confessed to Alyona
  about Polina.

Robert Desnos Finds His Sleep Medicines...

It is not bragging to finally come clean so that I might make a
   new start.

All that karma from a former life began to invade the way
   I kissed Sofia last night, having thought my past finally
   behind me.
How could I have believed the caves of the body? How could
   I have thought they held the seeds that I most need?

George Kalamaras

Jacques Cousteau Was a Splendid Blue Shadow

Stretch the displaced vertebral column you find in a fish.
Ask of it the means and the way. The committeeless committee.

I caress the beginning of an insult.
You draw back the air and speak the wedding guts of your sister's womb.

Still, it will always be a familiar regret astonishing my mouth.
I grew up that way, always afraid of what air I might speech.

There alone, inside the thorn of a cactus, the sharks are rumbling.
Jacques Cousteau was a splendid blue shadow.

My father was a hurricane. My mother, three fish sewn into the body of a blood pheasant.
Don't ask me to explain the meanderings of the sea, which somehow keep murmuring my mouth. Their way *into* my mouth.

If you want the truth, I'll tell you to go ask Kabir.
Lie inside one of his rug weavings, which somehow map starlight deadening an ear.

Ask Hafiz. Ask Leonard Bernstein. Ask Mike Tyson who keeps blow-boxing his shadow.

Jonah lived inside the belly of a whale. The whale lived inside him.

George Kalamaras

The Psychoanalysis of Fire

Those were the days of the psychoanalysis of an egg.
I saw the laboratory assistant cuddle a rat, cooing to it softly,
 before injecting it with yellow fever.

Sure, I'd been assigned to ghostwrite the autobiography of a
 pot of oolong tea.
But I found it less than forthcoming, even when I sat with it
 and drank it seductively.

There were bees in my mouth. Ancient texts uncovered from
 caves. Sophist explanations for the larger size of the right
 hand. The shyness of the foot.
There were blueprints for unknown buildings. Storms
 that had been destroyed. Diagrams for breathing, with
 instructions for how to reclaim the moon.

When the mailman arrived, I asked why he was carrying the
 weight of so many worlds.
When Jehovah's Witnesses came to the door, I told them I'd
 already been saved by a storm door with a good strong
 lock.

So, it was Bachelard who said, *At the center are the seeds; at the
 center is the engendering fire.*
So, like all things saved, it was Brother Antoninus who wrote
 a book of poems called *The Engendering Flood.*

Sure, he was William Everson at the time.
Of course, one name becomes another when passed plant to
 plant from the giraffe's tongue.

Robert Desnos Finds His Sleep Medicines...

I decided to move to an area of consciousness not previously
   mapped.
I hired a guide, but she deserted me halfway there.

I lay in the long grass of this new territory, hiding in the
   canebrake bending toward the river.
I decided to do nothing but count the freckles on a single stalk
   that had been too long in the world, blistered in wind,
   bowing beneath the fierce, fiery sun.

George Kalamaras

Centuries of My Any-Human-Pain

During the season of asthma, the pulse might become a
   yellow color, difficult of breath.
The thigh and hip become transformational properties.

Still, a steady rain might overturn an iron lantern.
Bite off the head of a silkworm and feel your own self swoon.

I approach the woozy end of my unmanifest mouth.
Words like a house of cards fall every which way.

The tea harvest, I learned, had advantages for the rural women
   of China.
A rebellion by religious zealots soon became a perfect
   specimen of large-leaf tea.

I don't know any more than that.
Like you, I just woke after a long breakfast.

The foreign presence of azaleas catapulted the season into
   Manchurian court power.
Authorities in Kolkata were displeased with the competition
   emanating from the north.

This mouth of mine has struggled with its tongue, tasting
   many centuries of any-human-pain.
So many poems were written as tributes to celestial events
   and the murdered mud within them.

Waiting for Your Echo to Enlarge Me

So we engaged in a brilliantly laconic conversation.
Less could be more, you told me, as I stood waiting for your
    echo to enlarge me.

Times were when I had been.
There were women I loved, dressed in taffeta and thin cotton
    wind.

Separation between footnotes seemed essential.
It was always the small print that seemed to trip me up, one
    way or another, whether the numbers unfolded in sequence
    or not.

Happiness could be the flesh of an owl, brilliant in moonlight.
The fluffed feathers are an emboldenment of all the unsaid
    three a.m. trains still groaning in my chest.

Rain in my hair. Leaves in the gutters of the throat.
A temporal exaltation could be sleep moss. In love.

In this rancorous weather, I should prepare a journey to the
    interior.
The gods would be generally approachable, I knew. If there
    were gods.

Scraps of Said in the Infinite Dark

Unreliable Narrator

How does the reader ultimately become a guide, not a
 companion?
After reading Malcolm Lowry's *Under the Volcano*, I knew
 I could never trust anyone again, even the pale green
 raincoat of my mother.

In one life, I grew up in the Hamburg brothels with Brahms.
I learned the word *brassiere* before *brazier*—the comfort of its
 warming calm.

I entered the monastery as "an interested observer."
The eyes had walls and could not see me.

You ask whether I am offended by a sudden seize of rain.
You decide to take me on a well-deserved vacation to a remote
 island with constant sun and a seemingly welcoming
 beach.

We knew that at least one of us was an indisputable liar. That
 we should never trust someone who regularly ate rain
 fragments on a cracker, as if they were caviar.
When Robert Desnos was expelled from the group, we knew
 the Period of Hypnotic Sleeps had come to a halt. That the
 sacristy of the mouth, as we knew it, had come to an abrupt
 and most sorrowful close.

George Kalamaras

In the Time of Borges and Calm

Then I awoke as a splinter of dawn in the arms of a young
 mother from Argentina.
I cried and cried and pissed my pants. She said soothing
 things to me, singing village folksongs with gentle coos.

There was a murmuring of milk. Wind in the pampas. Cows
 lowing in moonlight.
I grew calm at her soft brown breast and was certain I wanted
 more.

Then time stood dead.
Part of me was scarred, beyond repair.

I turned to climbing trees, to wrestling birds from the chest of
 a jaguar.
I learned how to count to twelve so that I could watch my life
 pass, hour by hour.

Someone read me a poem. Then the stories of Aesop. Then
 the biography of a wolf.
Newspapers came to claim what common sense I had.

I learned to recite the alphabet.
But I dwelled time and again on the first letter of everyone's
 name.

There was *M*, of course, for Mother and her milk. And *E*,
with her electric schoolyard voice. And *K & L*, who even
into my adulthood, had been forever kind and loving.
And they all came—these and others—to know me as *Aleph*,
the lonely letter I heard and was and upon which I seemed
to dwell.

And the libraries of Buenos Aires settled their dust and lent
me books, as if I were stung by bees or remained full of
cemetery madness.
And I once saw the man, Borges, himself, who stopped one
startling moment one afternoon as I entered a department
store behind him. And he kindly held the door for me.
One wind-struck instant. As if forever asking my name.

George Kalamaras

Mizzle

The perfect cave of dead regret is enclosed in an astonishing
   tongue.
Yesterday's Java sparrow survived the living vines surging its
   blood.

I asked my mother before she left the body if she would be my
   mother forever.
As she slept ever more slowly, there was a most normal world
   just a few breaths away.

Landforms and prairie grass call out to the black swallowtail.
The Maumee River's path from Fort Wayne, Indiana, to
   Defiance, Ohio, is so tortuous that settlers estimated the
   water took 160 miles just to travel the 100.

How might the poems of Yvan Goll make up to Paul Celan,
   begging for forgiveness, keeping him from that final leap
   from the bridge?
What parts of our mouth do we wish to wash out and rinse
   away?

I looked in the mirror and asked myself if I would be myself
   forever.
Don't forget that birds bear the enrichment of a thousand
   years.

Robert Desnos Finds His Sleep Medicines...

Sure, evolution is one thing, but toenail clippings suggest we sometimes grow beyond ourselves.
I once met a sadhu in Banaras who told me the rain was *not* the rain. That the Ganges we sat near and meditated by was a command to peer into ourselves and break the mirror. To watch the pieces float away. Forever.

George Kalamaras

Concessionary Recompense

I lived regret one farmland at a time.
Seasons enriched my fear in which only the dead survived.

Nightmares sponge open my iron voice.
Nests thrown aside are dirtied by my verse.

There is a pained smell famous as burnt weather.
So much of my past is as arbitrary as eel bites from the sea.

Jellyfish shadow my failure and my silk.
One form of familiar upset will reveal nothing.

When might an unexpected staircase float into my life and
 become the Suez Canal?
Woodchips in a glass call forth the Black Forest?

Closing your eyes into the night is the birth of a terrible
 telephone of trees.
For sixty-eight years I have been trying to call myself home.

My Vocabulary Did This to Me

We stayed hours, killing the warm miles behind us.
*Animals move and plants vegetate, oysters and tumbleweeds
    notwithstanding,* she told me, stroking the tender of her left
    earlobe.

But whatever internal sensation might require our animal
    noise, silence seemed best.
Moreover, upon closer inspection, an occasion of small
    openings gave pause.

Consider, that is, the egg sacs of the female bolas spider.
Consider the contents of a dead cow's throat. Bits of flesh left
    in the crow's beak.

Ask your ears if they have spoken enough.
If the eye fluid dampening a star might make it spin. Eternally.

All of my attention might lend itself to yours.
See how storms across the Sargasso Sea bolster one another
    and make fear the coast.

I learned to speak at times as if I were centuries old.
Remember how much Jack Spicer learned just from
    translating *Beowulf*?

There are green sea monsters and minute poisonous spiders
    that *did this to me*.
I looked up from my life into the eyes of the dead and said so.
    Again and again.

George Kalamaras

Elongation of the In-Between

I don't know anymore. Even the flattest lines somehow carve
    my heart.
Ask of me, slantwise through the throat, and you will find
    scrolls there, unearthed near the Dead Sea.

Near the salt craves of that sea, the end of the world is the end
    of something dear.
Throughout history, everyone—I have read—has had at least
    one nightmare sometime in their life of the moon splitting
    open like an oak before falling to earth with a thud.

Don't you remember? I know. I, too, think it hurts to be human.
Don't tell me about Sophocles and the tragedy of the human
    heart.

Don't repeat, backwards, the names of the salt-dead. The
    agony of the ants bitten into a life, colony-wise and drunk.
Repeat, please, only the middle names of Vicente Aleixandre.
    Miguel Hernández. Julio Cortázar.

Then recite the first and last names of the moon.
Then recite the names of Édouard Roditi's hamsters. The
    location of Richard Hugo's diseased and discarded left
    lung. The whereabouts of all the verbs Jack Spicer repeated
    as he tried to remember the blisters between each word in
    García Lorca's poems.

How many times have I said the word *heart* in the last
   thirteen minutes, forty-three seconds?
How many lives have I lived and died in that time? In the time
   it takes the in-between to elongate? To bleed one word
   into another—and thrive?

George Kalamaras

No One Persecuted a Single Word

Ask a fire ant the way home to the deserts of Namibia.
Locate its solar plexus as you might the exoskeleton of your
 own breathing.

Breathe. Breathing. Breathed. You know the insect dark as you
 might this cord of moonlight across your back.
Consider the towel sockets, the washrag joints, the calcium
 deposits of fine Egyptian cotton you cannot excrete.

Shall we travel to Harbin and replenish the ponies? Attract a
 Kyushu rooster somehow displaced in Siberia during the
 Russo-Japanese War?
Shall we seemingly but not quite? Shall we why we are here,
 now, as we tenuously approach our late sixties and miss a
 word here and there?

Too much of me is lagging behind, word by word, even in
 what's skipped, afraid to catch up.
I have broken the glass panels through which I might glimpse
 you. Spoken the electrical charge. Instructed the lamppost
 not to falter, even if it displays a frozen phrase that
 suggests, *Contained fire resembles the humid spirit.*

Even in February, most events take place in February.
We ate melons and meat in the open-air market, steam
 cutting from our throats like Quarter-Horse maneuvers
 through manure.

No one pranced but the ponies.
No one persecuted a single word.

Scraps of Said in the Infinite Dark

In this way, a week was a month. A month, a year. A year, the struggle for cosmic efficacy.
Everyone was delighted to take a very long time to try to say the phrase, *We were on our way to the mountain when heat lightning ignited us, and we imagined our spine a pillar of fire.*

Of course, it was a metaphor.
Of course, the spokes of the wheel slowed as if an ice shelf freshly adrift.

Then she told us what was wrong and right with the way we talked.
Then she said, *Sure enough, a few moments of pure love can be as indecipherable as wind in the bent water lilies of the throat.*

Honestly, my ears hurt.
Frankly, even the tooth into which I had sunk.

The streets were deserted, of course, and a vast silence encouraged the trees.
Wind from the pines abandoned all hope of displacing each and every needle into the tortoiseshell ground.

I decided to book passage on the Star of India after it was re-rigged into a salmon hauler for the Alaska-to-California Route.
I sat midnights on the deck, imagining the wingspan of manta rays below the surface, pulsing there through the infinite dark where no lightning, no mouth, could reach.

George Kalamaras

Now We Return to Sorrow

It is not without significance that we return to sorrow.
Give us this day our daily pain, and forgive us our laughter.

According to temple tradition, contemplation is the opposite
　of doubt.
Come to me in the Kyoto garden. Circumambulate with me
　each of the fifteen rocks in their gravel beds at dawn.

This is how I learned to practice circular breathing.
Each step on the stones offers another leap forward?

This is how I learned to tell time, eradicating the fraudulent
　pose of the clockface.
When one moment folds into another, we are asked to bust
　then burn all the accordions.

Recall with me, I beg you, the outline of a temple bell.
It is not without sorrow that sound arrives to remind us of the
　wholeness of all we have yet to become.

Separation of the Primal Pneuma

Such customs bring us to a decorative bookcase only moths might apprise.
Such weather might postpone death and carefully align our might.

But will the Milky Way always keep for us the cosmic crack ajar?
Might we misspeak and say something so wrong we damn ourselves to lifetimes of water and bones?

I was busy writing a biography of the hermit T'ao Ch'ien.
But I couldn't get past the first sentence that argued the book was really an autobiography of my previous life as an enigmatic parvisis from Yunnan Province.

Such confusion attempts to clarify the rigorous development of a poem?
Who, among us, has not begun to write about someone or some*thing* only to realize we are, in the end, writing about ourselves?

Why did the Primal Pneuma separate into *yin* and *yang*?
Other roles plagued me, as if I were the bridegroom of a distinguished gnat.

I only ask that when you look at me, please enumerate the willow branches about me.
Examine the curtains floating above the bed, and assure yourself that they are the opening and closing into a diffident but difficult rain.

George Kalamaras

Simply by Breathing

There is a Malaysian noon uncomfortable in its heat.
There is a denial of bones. Poems raided and expelled.

I roamed from a bee intestine into the foot of a jewel.
I made oyster pearls simply by breathing the lovely of your
    name.

Blood echoed in the spoken parts of evening.
So few people know that twilight also appears near dawn.

Improbable evening of walled flesh.
I would taste of you the newspaper storm of a charmed
    tenderness.

If I asked the lilacs the way to the woods, whose face would I
    find?
If the card game was fixed, would eternity break, or would my
    love for you return unharmed?

Bachelard Finds Himself Beneath His Own Floorboards and Realizes the Rain in His Gut Is an Epiphany

The Amazonian rainforest had been depleted for decades by blowdarts of disparate thought.
It kept waiting for the Blue Nile to merge with the White. For rain clouds to migrate from Mesopotamia. For the agony of defeat to be cradled *by* defeat.

It was sad to see Brahms picking sea lice from the left ear of his hound dog.
But when he cuddled with her winter nights near the fire a new intermezzo seemed to emerge and write itself.

Rain in the gutter seemed to seep into the house, down into the floorboards.
Everywhere we looked, things were opening up; there was what Gaston Bachelard called a *poetics of space*.

The rainy season in France. Cold but no snow. Bachelard pondered the puzzling cleavage of the sexes.
Prior to leaving the body, he ensured that his daughter, Suzanne, would become a mathematician and philosopher. Which she did, developing phenomenological and epistemological research of the highest world order. With a candle she placed into the fleshless chest of her father, crying out his name.

George Kalamaras

I Beg Robert Desnos to Heal Me

Yes, it hurts to be human.
I have written the tender parts of my wrist, exposing the
    panther's slow kiss of snow.

Over and over I have said *this*. I have said *that*.
You have heard whatever it is you have wanted to kill.

Sometimes an unexpected flirtation makes us feel young
    again, even in our late sixties.
Sometimes it comes from the sway of a sycamore. The bowing
    of eelgrass.

Even plants and trees are erotic.
But I didn't need to say that since I just showed it.

Why don't I follow my own instruction? Seek my own advice?
After all these decades of speech, I am still following my
    words wherever they want to go.

I thought about William Stafford. How easily dead he seems.
I heard Jack Spicer calming me all the way from Mars.

I bit off more Vicente Aleixandre than I could lose.
I courted the cliché, bathed in the right-way-wrong, certain
    that Miguel Hernández was there with his Franco-
    fractured heart.

I have learned more than I could weep.
That's one reason I turn to trees for sexual release.

Robert Desnos Finds His Sleep Medicines...

If Yvonne George—with whom Desnos was smitten—was there in her dancehall garb. If Youki Desnos. If the unnamed pleasure that is my name.
Bring me the sleep medicines, Robert Desnos. Take my hand and read only the good parts of my palm. Talk to me from the other side of my world.

EVERY WORD I SPOKE

Bingo

Sleep forms dominate my dead.
René Crevel, René Daumal. René Char.

Try a game of bingo.
Cover five such squares in a row.

Add René Magritte. And your great uncle Theodorosios
 Demopoulos.
Watch the sky fall apart and lament its bird droppings into
 you all the way from the village of Solaki in Messenia.

Okay, you tell me again to shut up. To speak straight or not at
 all. To finally put a stork in it.
Say that you have listened to the paddy-field wingbeats of my
 tongue long enough. That you have lifted many swarmings
 through the rice crops. Listened long if not hard.

Monsoon textures to language may dominate.
The tongue might quicken and moisten and speak.

All the sleep medicines of Robert Desnos are hiding.
He is at the café again talking to his friends in his sleep.
 Slumped over a croissant. Translating a dream. Somehow
 slurping his coffee. Unable to wake up.

George Kalamaras

The Long Ride

So we came away from there thinking we had not yet been.
So the drops of bees' blood on the pillow must have come
    from the way our ear had heard many lifetimes in the dark.

For a long time, I have been floating lengthwise through the
    chest cavity of a quite marvelous whooping crane.
This beautiful species streamed to Nebraska all the way from
    South Africa, nesting—as it flew over—in my six-year-old
    Indiana ear.

What sad thing has fallen from us from the moment we fly
    from the womb and take our first breath?
Just in the course of writing that sentence, I tell you, I have
    died seventeen and one-third times.

When the tiny locust leaves its shell, it is a whitish color,
    clouded with fog-ridden red.
Its claw, scooped out like a spoon, is what the gray locust is
    using to keep pickaxing my brain.

I see the way she bites the soil and remember my months in
    the womb.
Breathing under water, Cousteau told us, *is an attractive notion.*

By the end of April, January had become February, and young
    grubs were imprisoned in many cages.
Yes, even the moon counts my arm hair as it sleeps.

Robert Desnos Finds His Sleep Medicines...

When I woke into my morning tea, I saw Mongols riding in from the thirteenth-century steppes across Eurasia.
They carried swords that gleamed, told bawdy jokes, and somehow around the evening fires assured me of the necessity of the long ride to find someone to whom to tell my story.

George Kalamaras

Black Threads of Gold

Now we come to the study of death in the chest.
We come to condolences. We come to regret.

I remember the first dead person I ever saw.
Third grade. The stiffness of the world lying there, as if inside me.

André Malraux wrote about the initial use of mustard gas in the First World War.
I can still hear the wailing of a baboon from thirty-three years ago at the San Diego Zoo.

The famous poet seemed to compliment my reading some years back, saying it felt like *anything* could happen in my poems at just about any time.
"The Sect of the Old Ones" goes back to Padmasambava— and so do honeybees circling the body of the yogi whose hut I sat in thirty years ago in Banaras.

That was the time when Freud was feuding with Jung. When Jung wondered why Bachelard examined fire through psychoanalysis, not archetypes.
I recently came upon the dickey I wore to that first funeral and could not discard it, somehow cherishing its fifty-nine years of black thread, even as it lay dormant all this time in a drawer.

We are connected to more than what we are connected to?
You examine the encyclopedia to get a fix on the letter *D*— how I doublespeak and don't?

Robert Desnos Finds His Sleep Medicines...

The great paradox of opium eaters is that when they eat they take in no nourishment.

I have a painting of Padmasambava on the wall of my study. Even the gold of the frame cannot confiscate or contain the music from the many lives he brings. The many lives therein.

George Kalamaras

Anywhere We Step

Say the Great Barrier Reef awoke in our bones.
Say the night sky revolved in sockets of sleep.

I was in love with a lamp inside a gorgeous woman's thigh.
Everywhere we touched there was light darkening light.
    Starlight in the rain-soaked leaves.

You think me obsessed with the Macedonian dead?
You cry out that my sword and shield are remnants of a
    strange sickly speak?

There is a marvelous hallucination in the kerosene rag, fragile
    as a universe.
There are blossoms of noise chasing the echo beyond the wall.

Anywhere we step could be an argumentative storm.
I ate sycamore leaves and the bones of crows as one way to
    save the grace of my name.

Clockwork

I doubt it was she who came to me last night.
It was butterflies I tasted. Moths. Bees' blood in the throat.

Abandoned hour of black mirrors.
The tea kettle tells tales of cruel moons asleep.

Complete border of corporeal passports.
We crossed an immense river in a quite big rain.

Odd, the hairy poem following me lifetime to lifetime.
Odd, the aching groin and passionate shoes.

Having received the honor of birth, I cried to my mother at
 the moment we met to let her know the extent of my pain.
The length of the journey had been a dark mountain range with
 caravans of nomads and the splendid harnesses of yaks.

Later, years later, I sat in an abandoned house and watched
 spring arrive.
Yes, they taught me how to tell time: The big hand was on my
 shoulder, the little hand on my throat.

George Kalamaras

Home

I honestly don't know how to let you see the real you.
I keep a pet parakeet in my jacket pocket, but all you see is a silk handkerchief.

Yesterday, they floated an air balloon downwind as if it were an unexploded bomb.
That's how I feel about most poems I read—but only the good ones.

If I told you I dream of Vicente Aleixandre most nights—that I am his nurse, that he and I play poker at the sanatorium until he gets well—would you think me insane?
How many images of animals on fire in the intestines would it take for you to recognize what dream your dreams most long to hold?

I decided to retire from teaching. To return to school and finally study anthropology.
I wanted to learn all I could about the languid lull of the dead.

I was sure a hand in the bird meant blood and guts.
I'd so long counted on the feathers in my chest as a possible way out.

I knew that if I could decode the deeper layers of Rumi that I might gleam one day like freshly polished copper.
I slept each night and dreamed I'd returned to my dead mother's home. Which was her body. Her bones. In which I swam in a solution of starlight and well-being disguised as well water housed in the mouths of the dead.

Every Word I Spoke

We had set out that lifetime through boreal forests and
 perishable feasts.
I swear, I ache this time around because of the bogs I entered
 and the tamarisk steppes that taunted us.

You want to know why it is continuously raining inside my
 throat?
You can barely look at me, for fear you might seek yourself?

The dervish had made a generous request.
Thereupon, we approached mirrors with delicacy and shame.

Familiarity with the other side of madness makes me whirl.
Not a day passes without some spiritual tragedy that calls the
 body into question.

On the contrary, there was cemetery madness every time I ate
 cooked food.
I started to advance cautiously from camp but forgot that the
 kerosene was embedded in my spleen.

No wonder I couldn't see in the dark.
No wonder every word I spoke had already been spoken.
 Inside. Unto me and through.

George Kalamaras

Traveling North

They would nudge me as if I were a methodical man.
I suspected this contempt, a cigarette clothed in ravenous
  squalls of snow.

I didn't need healing.
I didn't require their pity.

I needed a word, pure—for once—as the driven alphabet.
Place the *p* of *panache* anywhere in a word, perhaps at the
  back to give it *pop*, or *plop*, or even *chomp*.

When you approach the pole, even the compass of its own
  letters goes mad.
Watch, with awe, the needle of my life go blind.

Did I say I didn't need healing?
Would you pity me, please, for pitying no one but *me*?

So it is that the blood flow from my heart is a walrus wailing
  at the air hole at the strike of the harpoon, the taper of a
  seal-oil lamp sooting the roof of that which I most crave.
The texture of a rickety absence overloads even that most
  persistent scar I might call home.

Feeble eyelid rather than a tear grumbling down a freshly
  gessoed canvas.
Occupy the cavilings, the vague mortal distance between
  perfectly human confusion and how far north I may now
  need to be.

This, Our Family

Bloodlines thin as a fingernail.
Casual attack of electrocuted skin.

We might look north where their words invade, imagine
    clocks in our going mad.
We might be led down corridors of epilepsy, asking ourselves
    if it was really worth the handshake and the hug.

There are ways of foul connection.
There is a sacrifice—sometimes filthy—for the birdcage and
    the way.

Take my blind-beak self and counteract the feathers.
Drop a parachute from the plane—bundle of homeopathic
    medicines—and marvel at the almost-imperceptible arc of
    falling.

Bloodlines thick as ice picks in the brain.
This, our family, our flat mattress, our kingdom of cameras
    and hopeful sorrow and civilian animals connecting our
    secret bleed to the botfly on the flesh of a wall.

George Kalamaras

We Knew Something Good

We absorbed the wood of the splintered moon.
We moved inside the aching rain as one way to become tiny
    Surrealist suns.

There had been Magritte, of course. And Joan Miró.
There were also parts of Paul Klee transparent against
    raindrops on the sliding glass.

We were broody and worthless all afternoon.
We ate pizza every day topped with caramelized onions and
    sautéed eggplant.

We knew something good by the amount of pain it held.
We measured it by water. Restless water. By what was drank
    and what was drunk.

None of the verb tenses fit. None could be decided upon.
None of the tiny suns burst upon our chest as a notorious
    nest of gnats.

We searched for a tense called *the future past's future*.
Branching out backwards seemed the best approach.

Then we were summoned by an old green truck with a bed of
    sand and mud for ballast.
Would we ever be seen again, we wondered, on this route
    or that? Clear as a smeared shadow in the blowing rain
    turning to snow?

The Fifth Manifesto

We move through a beautiful urge of words.
There are streetlamps, antique tongues, lovers without
    mouths.

The moon filled the moth wings with illicit body smoke.
Everything I touched had somehow already touched me.

I asked the astrologer whether our mutual past might have
    something to do with the rise of Bolshevism in Tanzania.
She thought the past should stay in the future. That we
    should learn to let sleeping dogs experience flight.

One of the main points of Breton's public attack on Desnos
    in the *Second Manifesto* was Desnos's practice of drinking
    food and eating water.
The story about his fondness for composing alexandrines was
    a metaphor to disguise Breton's gastronomical disgust.

Transparent feathers vibrate little-known cages.
We allow our association with knives to prepare the maps for
    our adventures East.

I woke unto the throat and asked about a beautiful deformity
    of quite cramping rain.
I have so often dreamed of walking out of my life.

George Kalamaras

It Takes More Than a Million Lives Just to Become Human

We were fortunate to find an embankment of snow to hunker down into.
We were lucky to wait out the blizzard and camp inside our own mouths.

In those days, I kept a notebook describing a series of man-made tunnels.
I was always looking for a way out of my moods. A way to shortcut the many incarnations it takes even after we finally become human.

The paradox of a luncheon of breakfast food should be evident.
If you read the poems chronicling Pierre Unik's journey from Surrealism to Marxism, it should be clear that the social contract of worms burrowing earth is both social *and* scientific.

Last night, I dreamt that the great Greek Surrealist Nikos Engonopoulos put down his poems and paintbrush and came to me as a talking tree.
We stood on the banks of the Maritsa, reciting fragments from Sappho into a collage that spoke the broken moon, describing men being born from a woman's rib. The rib, a piece of solidified sound bees make when they mate with fire.

We were fortunate to have the holy fragments.
We were lucky to have body hair with which to hear one another's response.

Then I spent two days—maybe three—alone below great shovelsful of worm castings on blessèd Mount Athos.
One by one, the Hesychasts filed by, telling me that if I wanted to stay I must grow a beard like them in the Orthodox way. Soon as I could.

George Kalamaras

Aspects of the Almost-Arriving Moon

I can't lie about traveling those months with Paul Brunton.
No, I did not ghostwrite *A Search in Secret India*. I sat with
   him evenings, though, by the Ganges, fishing for lost parts
   of our dream worlds that had merged and sunk into the
   river.

The sun bled aspects of an almost-arriving moon.
Sunset in the mouth reminds me how little time we actually
   have to speak.

Ray tells me this. John tells me that.
Larry is in California, reading *Nadja* backwards into a mirror
   so that I might sleep.

What if it was you rather than a Czech medical student
   who found Robert Desnos stumbling on the road after
   Buchenwald, delirious and half-dead from typhus?
What if there'd been no bed to lay him in. No rose for
   the nurse, Alena Tesarova, to give him. The rose he lay
   clutching before he left the body to enter the dream he
   always knew had been hovering just inches above his
   poems those years of the hypnotic sleeps.

Honestly, even I get confused by my own mouth.
It is as if Dino Campana did odd jobs, like his circus
   tumbling, there, below my tongue, those years he wandered
   after his poetry in the asylum.

I can't lie about Paul Brunton and me sharing a cigar at the
   cremation ghat, later smoking starlight as it entered the
   mouths of the dead.
Moon in the gill of a gold carp. Somehow, the Ganges travels
   all the way to both the Wabash and the Kankakee.

How was I reborn so quickly after cholera wasted the moon
   leaves of my gut?
How did I ever get here from there?

The Meticulous Mice of the Lantern-Lathed Tongue

After Thirty-Two Years

I have been visited by an entire swarm of birds.
Look up, into the sky, and see how autumn shaves the
 farmlands.

His list of students is an impressive one: Mahler, Liszt, Willie
 Mays.
How the music of Robert Fuchs influenced the 1962 World
 Series is a topic for a dissertation on the cavilings of
 sound.

Callomania is another.
Like calling into the camerated chambers of your lover's heart.

Look down, into the sky, spoiled there in a muddy pool.
Bathe in the visitation of a thousand swarms of bees.

Study the box score of your life.
Sit mornings. Sit mornings with Jack Spicer at Gino & Carlo's
 bar and allow the sound. Allow the sound of all the stolen
 bases. All the foul balls he might repeat.

Come back. Come back to Fort Wayne, Jack. Every student.
 Every student of mine is pleading.
I am about to retire my turtleneck and tweed.

Oh, the words we work, working us. There have been too
 many and not enough.
There is a Carthaginian Peace. The Roman spears assured us
 that all the elephants are dead.

George Kalamaras

What Makes the Repetitions in Our Head Is Only an Interruption in the Death Dream of Robert Desnos

That was the winter we had drunk nearly all of the melted snow.
Glands located in the cloaca might have been another way of weeping.

Instead of remaining in the stone hut, we refurbished the wind in our throat.
It might be more conducive to be a possible trapper, to have invented—then destroyed—the steel-jawed leghold trap in the 1840s.

Some things are lost, even when found.
The flightless moa of New Zealand may be extinct, but each of the nine species might help us count our fingers close to ten, might be another way to experience the City of Nine Gates the Upanishads describe.

Sure the violet rays of the rainbow are the ones that cause the most repetitive chemical actions.
But the history of coffee as a sleep mantra could easily be described in a series of unexpected naps.

I have been traveling a long time in the exoskeleton of a termite from Borneo.
I have wanton and asked-for and blessèd be my mouth.

When Robert Desnos boarded the *Titanic*—from a Paris
 café—for an interrupted trip to Fiji, his dream talk began
 to warm the icy waters. Subside in the tide pools.
There were violent bursts of flame that emanated even from
 his toes.

Ask me to speak more plainly, if you must, but know it may
 be with dead words of the long-dead dead.
So much birth is birthed from birth to birth that it makes the
 repetitions in my head spin. The Tibetan prayer wheels
 revolve. The arms of the midwife ache.

George Kalamaras

There Seemed Nowhere Else to Go

Comforted by the efficacy of human kindness, we revealed all our tenterhooks.
There was only a solitary bee housed in the mouth.

There seemed nowhere else to go except deeper into our own blood.
Yes, I had read a book on indigenous sign language, but I could not find a sign for, *Please forgive me my mouth*.

Or had I meant, *Please forgive me, my mouth?*
The world can appear and disappear inside even the softest curling pearl of a comma.

What might it mean to survive a hospitable frontier?
How might we conjure and Conestoga and confidential our words?

Every afternoon I drove by the Primitive Baptist Church in Fort Wayne, Indiana.
And every day, I imagined a primordial Christianity somehow practiced centuries *before* the birth of Christ in the rainforests of the Congo. On the banks of the Euphrates. In a thatched hut in Borneo.

It seems unlikely that Alvaro and Gene are still alive.
I came away from both of their memorials knowing they would remain with me. Here. Now.

Some things are true and not true at the same time.
Everything I have said here is a lie.

Brahms by Firelight

That was when the great jaw of music clamped down around
    us.
There were dust mites in my beard. Swamp salt. A way of
    speaking in which words splayed themselves open to reveal
    something lonely and long.

Response to a clear night reminded me of weeks speaking
    Bangala, even in Ujiji.
Creeper vines seemed displaced when not in my chest but
    crawling up a leadwood tree or a marula.

Among the daily periodicals, I favored *The Times of London*,
    though the promotion of servitude concerned me.
I asked of the wind more than the wind could provide, even as
    the tiny movements of its mice enthralled me.

We all have something from which we're hiding, I thought, *some
    grinding in the gut we set out to forget.*
When I read books about the Arctic, I chill it near my bone.
    When I break bread with it, it aches to invade me.

Nothing seemed to help but Brahms. Especially by firelight.
The third movement of the Third Symphony rises up from
    the freshly tilled earth into something whole in my throat.

I could return to Zimbabwe or Ujiji. Even Brazzaville if I held
    the right song as a feral displacement of bones.
I could ask of it to heal me in the way only the hurt of living
    could possibly do.

George Kalamaras

I Would Tongue of It and Plead

We must meet in the oracle.
We most meet when one of us but two.

Let me call you *Ramani—beautiful woman.*
Let me gently tongue that narcotic mole on your neck.

There was an immensely important moment.
It was *exactly* like every other I had ever bled.

Tea in the morning and toast.
Burnt crust showeth me my shame.

We most often, and we likely.
We hide of it and speech.

Seek not *The Book of Perfect Hygiene.*
Inside me, it is written in sacred Sanskrit, *Two left hands are not doubly dirty.*

Let me call you *Bhoomika—the Earth—*even *Calm-Caressed Storm* or *Whooping-Crane-My-Heart.*
Let me of that mole complete myself in your moist brown Maharashtrian skin.

Robert Desnos Finds His Sleep Medicines...

You cooked foods for me that evening, somehow entering me
 through the stew.
Let me call you *every name imaginable*. In the morning in your
 eyes. In my gentle. In your shy. In your drowsy-eyed brush-
 back of hair. In the touch of your lip to the spoon during
 the meal we share. Sounding your vowel throughout me.
 Sounding me most alive.

George Kalamaras

The Meticulous Mice of the Lantern-Lathed Tongue

I remember that birth during the Edo period. The smell of
 horse lather. Of ruts in the road. Of women squatting in
 the field. Men relieving themselves against a wall.
In those days, everyone's hair was on fire.

The emptiness the deutzia bush breathed into me was a sack
 of fine flour.
Someone spoke in words that resembled thinly laid noodles.

Another spoke as if a tree was continuously in bloom.
Someone removed her ear and laid it on a plate of ash.

Then it was as if time stood running.
As if, still, the world was revolving around the moon.

As if time itself was time.
And the lanterns in the heart blazed in ways from which even
 the horses sank.

Lord knows, the time of the tongue was the time of the
 tongue tied to the mouth.
Lord knows, there was an owl on fire inside the nightmares of
 tiny twitching mice among the kerosene cuts of the world.

In those days, I feared I had only one birth to endure,
   fashioning silk and a finely shaved leg from every breath I
   shook.
I looked to the feet of the dishonored women in the red
   quarter in Yoshiwara as if they stood for something others
   could not see. As if they were my life.

George Kalamaras

Fire-Eater

At a time like this, I should eat poisonous snowberries.
I should regurgitate the book, the endpapers embossed with
   the image of a heron eating a watery weed.

Weeping as though from a bitter dose of verbs, I grieved
   autumn's quick-turning ash, seeds in my belly scraped raw,
   unable to bleed.
I stopped along the road near the house of Lord Minamoto,
   moved to perform any proper activity, even to ritualize the
   picking of a snowberry or relieving myself discreetly in the
   weeds.

He had died. A few months before that, he'd been alive.
A few months after, he was a ghost, fire-breaking his pavilions
   to ash.

Yes, I lived some years as a sheep tramping through the mud
   of hen-sex and rut.
I had lived lives as a Lord, as a geisha pouring tea, even as the
   silk lip of a parlor bell.

Your sisters must all be at home, either he or I or the sheep had
   inferred, back-scratching against a fencepost to quicken
   the tumble of a tick. *Hand me the taper you must have
   bequeathed, so I can carve the dark back unto you.*
In those days of silk kimonos and hair pinned to reveal her
   makeup, nothing moved me like the fire-eater who arrived
   one day from the West in search of a mouth. A place to lay
   her tongue, she said, and do her work.

A Brief History of Mirrors

Now we come to the age of sparrows in the throat.
When I was a child I spoke rain slantwise into this tree and that.

There was a Japanese bowl from the Kamakura period.
Even then, it held the roundness of now.

Count with me here the number of owl feathers fastened to the moon.
Ask your own mouth to consider the quiet movements of a river refusing monotony.

At times we appear released, as if breaking with a great force.
We shyly and reflect upon and—of course—away.

There was a mirror incident in Borneo that did and did not involve me.
So it is with the water buffalo that brought parasites from the watering hole into my lover's arms, and brought her—after many years—back into mine.

George Kalamaras

Yes, Our Internal Organs Knew Better

Before a general rendezvous of superfluous caution, we knew
    someone had to have an answer.
We set out a packet of saltines. Prayed to Tristan Tzara.
    Pledged our lives to Dada.

You might think it weird to be so enamored with the
    unsayable.
But imagine Captain Cook, boiled and flayed after being
    killed for trying to take prisoner a Hawaiian chief.

All our internal organs knew better.
Even our body hair.

Coconuts and breadfruit might appear to be mountains in
    New Guinea.
Mix a crumb of wheaten bread with a Jerusalem artichoke,
    and imagine your life grown sweet.

Try to understand that if we grew up with horses, we will
    always be running up against the fence.
The problem becomes when our lives are barbed, and tetanus
    locks lockjaw in for good.

All of which brings me back to the Dada plays Hugo Ball
    wanted to produce and take to Tokyo.
One wonders if they could have prevented Iwo Jima and the
    incarnate slaughter, even hookworm in the prisoners who
    built a bridge over the River Kwai.

But if the film was fictional, the construction of the Burma
 Railway—the *Death Railway*—was not.
We could explore the globe with a sheaf of great jungle space.

We could echo and carnage and silt.
We could stand on the stage babbling the one word not in
 anyone's vocabulary, asking for it to be anointed in ways
 that might allow the mouth. That might punctuate a
 phrase. A delirious past with a promulgation of tongues
 tender yet torn.

George Kalamaras

Jacques Cousteau and the Dark Lengths of Rain

Now we come to the dark lengths of rain unfolding like unrepentant seasons.
We think of water. We return to the sea. We contemplate that two-thirds of an octopus's cognition lies outside its brain, in each of its eight probing tentacles.

What might a difficult case of psoriasis say about one's repressed emotions?
How might one's ergophobia be traced back to the long hours his mother put in at the paper mill when he was just five?

Yes, the world is breaking apart.
Of course, the air is thickening even as it thins.

Surely, the correct course of action might have something to do with opening one's own belly with a jackknife and inserting three crow feathers before sewing oneself back up.
Of course, even Jacques Cousteau had to admit that diving in the ocean deeps was a way to reenter the birth canal of his mother.

Now we ocean and wave and manta ray the winging deeps.
We confiscate the salt at the kitchen table of every so-called friend and sneak it home to press the granules into the tender places in our wrist.

Robert Desnos Finds His Sleep Medicines...

I have been traveling far too long through this life and that,
   the way wolves roam Lapland in winter in search of
   sustenance and an outcrop of mossy rock for sleep.
I can say with absolute confidence that my totem animal, the
   musk ox, preserves its energy in subzero winds by standing
   in a three-day blizzard perfectly still as it possibly can.

George Kalamaras

Kurosawa Sometimes Wept Inside Kawabata's Dream

Now we turn to the recesses of the mouth.
The darkness therein. The darkness we become.

Each word, a red-crowned crane rising through mist from the lowland swamp.
The way Dostoevsky lamented his lot in exile in Siberia.

The way Nikolai Gogol could never again wear his overcoat with pride.
The way Jack London kept mushing the dog team from this book to that.

Thus, the snow said unto him—unto them all—*Here, bleed into me so that you may see droplets of the pathway home.*
Thus, Kurosawa sometimes got confused, as if he wept inside Kawabata's dream.

Thus, the seven samurai were sometimes eight. Sometimes nine and a half, depending on the chakra count.
And no one. No one saw the same thing in the *Rashomon* woods of Akutagawa's sleep.

Yannis Ritsos remained under fervent house arrest on the island of Samos.
And ravens came, early each morning, to peck the eyes out of his poems.

Robert Desnos Finds His Sleep Medicines...

So, what has this to do with the pleasures of speak? With one
   tongue searching the Belovèd's mouth for what to say and
   how?
In other words, I must admit that I adore the way the width
   of her hips in the night.

Dostoevsky Trims His Nose Hair Prior to Bathing His Toes, I
   had read one evening. Aloud. Considering this the best
   book title of the year.
And I try my *own* form of weeping. Put it on like a damp,
   bland shirt. While reading the death agonies of Lorca,
   Vallejo, and Desnos.

While measuring the weight and waste of rain-soaked leaves.
So much autumn in an autumn leaf. So much silence in the
   words we speak.

George Kalamaras

Photo of Brahms on His Deathbed

Now all the prostitutes are asleep.
And your piano is finally quiet.

The third movement of the Third Symphony has closed.
All six minutes twenty seconds hold your nearly sixty-four years.

Like the sixty-fourth hexagram closing the *I Ching*, the water of these notes flows downhill, seeking a thatched hut, a hermit cave where the lament of all-night trains resounds.
And the soreness of water seeking water only grows increasingly hoarse.

There is a great blue heron with whooping cough scraping the canebrake.
And it has invaded my veins with a stalking for fish only 4:02 a.m. this morning can reveal.

If I had a kerosene lamp, I would carry it all the way to Hamburg and visit your birth bag.
I would kneel of it. Ask of it and pray. I would beg forgiveness for all I have never heard.

If I had a kerosene rag, I would wrap it round a pine board. Go all the way to Vienna and torch your deathbed.
I would ask the women from the brothels of your youth not to touch you—ever again—to simply let your childhood piano keys stalk the reeds and allow the swirling gnats of gentleman cigar smoke to settle and warm.

Robert Desnos Finds His Sleep Medicines ...

Now there are flowers abounding your head, blurring both
 your sorrow and your joy. Six hundred twenty blossoms.
And your beard, Johannes, is slow and combed, as if waiting
 for a great wind to startle your mouth. To stir the moths
 that are sure to come with dimming wings to measure your
 head. Feed the lamps.

George Kalamaras

Robert Desnos Finds His Sleep Medicines Beneath Bachelard's Floorboards

Another night of Brahms, sea lice, and worms working this Indiana dark.
I could live forever inside the chest cavity of a fallen sparrow.

The world is far away, even in its closeness.
There is an owl hooting in the pine in my backyard, speaking in code only both the moon and I know.

Those nights forty-one years ago when John and I read Vallejo together until three.
The Mingus stories Larry and I share by email at one a.m. or two, as if a train track in the chest.

Say André Breton didn't write *Nadja* after all but found it in the startling breath of a horse chestnut.
Say that when George Seferis emptied his pipe, what he pounded out was not ash but fractures of all the poems he could never quite speak.

Shoe and tobacco advertisements become intervals of desperate Chinese characters in Kunming.
In Indiana, I wanted every typeface in Cochin, but when I heard the word, all I could think was *Cochinchina*—an unfortunate exonym for part of Vietnam.

Robert Desnos Finds His Sleep Medicines ...

The guilt of colonialism is real, the giving of a name sacred as
    rock salt chunked into the possum struck at the side of the
    road.
Ask your owl friend and hear wind ruffle its wings as it tries
    to leave you for another tree. For the shivering woods of
    other words, less aggressive.

When Robert Desnos temporarily lost his voice one night,
    he hunted for it first in the brothels tucked among dark
    streets. Then in the folds of a croissant smothered in
    butter. Then finally beneath Bachelard's floorboards.
How beautiful the sleep medicines, he said, stroking his voice
    tenderly by kerosene lamp. *How lovely the Mother Night.*

Borges and the Library of Babel

Michael Mitsakis Thought That Every Six Was a Nine

Some have claimed I am as mad as Michael Mitsakis.
Some have searched the annals of Greek poetry to see if it was
    me and not Mitsakis locked all those years in the asylum.

I admit that I have measured the moment of my mouth
    against a fully dark moon.
I promise you that I have gone to the swamp many midnights
    to pray for the welfare of all sentient beings.

It has been a long slog to come up from my amoeba self into
    this fully human form.
I have served many midnights in the luminous rib of an owl,
    nourishing it with my mouse-bone self.

Yesterday, I read a news article in the local paper that said I
    have never existed.
It began, *Once upon a time, lightning came as thunder as words
    as a swarm of bees upon this man who supposedly visited our
    town.*

All I can say is study the poems of Robert Desnos, and you
    will find true love for termites and ants in his unrequited
    love for the dancehall singer Yvonne George.
If you go to the wall calendar, you will see that I have marked
    out the sixth day of every sixth week—just to see if I
    can get the year to add up to nine days in the river, nine
    months in my mouth.

George Kalamaras

Zorba the Greek

That dream where Nikos Kazantzakis comes to dance with
 me on a beach in Crete.
The part where Carlos Fuentes arrives and tells me Aura is the
 one I must love—both the young woman *and* the hag.

The sequence when Kawabata smokes a cigarette somehow
 through *my* mouth, not his.
Then Remedios Varo comes to settle all the birds that have
 taken refuge in my brain, Borges dressed in a skirt as her
 secretary with heels.

Dark lovely water I float into and through.
Whitmanesque in all my various mouths.

Then the urge to pee, and afterwards a deeper sleep calming
 me.
And I'm in a coffeehouse in Madrid, and Vicente Aleixandre
 arrives with the spine of some ancient sea creature from
 Mallorca.

God knows I love him and his primordial pain.
Lord knows he holds in his bowels the shadows of both Lorca
 and Hernández.

That part of my dream where Delvaux confides he's been
 painting worm castings, not women.
And Bachelard begs me not to fall asleep again beneath his
 floorboards.

Robert Desnos Finds His Sleep Medicines . . .

And all the poets named René approach, folded into one
 another—Crevel, Daumal, Char, and some janitor named
 René from Lucerne, who swears he adores poetry but
 wants to cleanse my mouth.
And Julio Cortázar hands me his cat to care for while he
 bakes bread—and somehow I don't sneeze, though
 Cortázar is actually outside in the pampas planting trees.

The wind, the wind, the terrible wind.
Vallejo keeps inscribing me into some book he carries, which
 is actually the body of a dead man.

And Arthur Waley rises from his deathbed at Highgate,
 where the curtains dance when he speaks—though he
 looks exactly like Baryshnikov. And translates *the body of a
 dead man* into *the folding doors of a corpse.*
And I'm puzzled, drinking tea with Tu Fu, who's also Rodney
 Dangerfield, but somehow I'm also in the garden playing
 cards with Lee Miller and Dora Maar.

And in a teahouse in Kyoto, Kawabata returns as Takahashi
 Shinkichi who's somehow a giraffe back in Crete strangely
 able to swim, wind from the long purple tongue of his
 Dada poems threatening to consume me.
And I'm on the beach again, but Kazantzakis is gone. The
 wind is gone. And the dark waters rise to the sound of the
 santouri. And I sense they are afraid of the dawn and the
 clarity of meaning it might bring.

George Kalamaras

At the Corner of Vallejo and Wang Wei

In middle years, I thought of Wang Wei's poem beginning *In my middle years* . . .
Consider the word *enigma*. Listen to a bird wing caught, mid-fall, in the chest.

Water buffalo urine weighs more than possum piss?
Soaked rice paddies are a measure of bloated yet cedar-scented bamboo?

Ask the weather if it possibly just might.
Conditions change, as our decades often do, especially as rain in our throat begins to mature.

Take your wife's hair delicately in your left hand, reciting minefields from your favorite Vallejo poem.
Smell it, comrade, for the dung stirrings of your own beating heart.

In late middle years, I am slow-eyeing the later years that may or may not lie ahead.
At sixty-eight, I still massage my joints, work my tongue each night into the ink-blue eggs of an immaculate blood pheasant.

Robert Desnos Finds His Sleep Medicines...

Dark across the heart. Shards of many caravans lumber and pass. A Gobi rat, a fire ant, camels whose humps slowly mimic Bactrian borders that refuse the moon.
In the murmuring moment and swarmings of the mouth, I am sharpened by all I have said. By what I have stumbled through. By what I have chosen not to reveal.

George Kalamaras

Borges and the Library of Babel

No one believes me when I say there's a cello in my gut.
Even the spectacled mountain rat can't seem to find its way
    out of the jungles of Malacca.

No one climbs trees anymore to hear the babble beyond, to
    test the waterfalls of Borneo and Sumatra for hidden glints
    of sound.
An excitable affidavit might be reintroduced into a forested
    way of weather where fog becomes rain when the
    temperature swells.

You ask that I be nice, that I return the tincture of benzoin
    since the canker sores have nearly broken.
You refuse my allotment of pain, calling on Borges and his
    magical library to draw the labyrinth into your own palm.

No one hears the violin in their throat, convinced it is an
    Arabic bee swarming in from Algeria. A dust storm in a
    hexagonal room. A floating staircase.
Even the night sky is shy of its own darkness.

I was given three potatoes yesterday at the farmer's market
    and instructed to make soup.
I was photographed hiding in my pocket a miniature copy of
    Gustave Courbet's painting *The Origin of the World*.

As the cello concerto drew to a close, there was a curtain that
    seemed to open even as it clothed.
There was a fabric so thin it blocked out the past while
    suggesting the curvature of the earth.

Robert Desnos Finds His Sleep Medicines...

I went home and reread every story by Borges that I could.
I kept one word on my tongue, coaxing clues from the sores in
 my mouth, repeating again and again—*world, world, world.*

George Kalamaras

A Quarter of an Hour to Search Within

Everywhere I turned, there were blackbirds in my chest.
I'm learning to stand on one leg. Like an egret confronting the
    dark. Like a sadhu in Banaras practicing austerities.

There is a physical power in most days of promised burning.
Halidom. A sacred oath. Oddments at the kitchen sink.

I began a thorough study of the Japanese tea ceremony.
I wanted to finally be beautiful. Like something about to die.

But whatever the aim, cosmic forces urged the honeybee
    home.
I combed my hair without a part, hoping to finally make a
    nest of things. Whole.

To single out a quarter of an hour to search within.
It is like the wishbone of the man-o'-war bird holding trade
    winds of the Caribbean intact. Even those from different
    directions.

Yes, samurai lived on fixed stipends.
How else can you measure protection and death?

Everywhere I turned, there were myna birds in my mouth,
    crowding out my words.
I opened the *I Ching,* exosculating it when no one was
    looking. Each kiss I gave it was somehow meant for me.

Every Word I Failed to Read

Then the whooping crane flew slantwise through my throat.
Then the passel of crows absorbed my body as my body
    absorbed their dark and all its sound.

Once, when I was young, I was very old.
Once, when I aged, it was the young of my tongue to which I
    clung.

Say I could and I couldn't.
Say I just might and maybe and more.

What a good idea to drink a glass of water.
What thought to go to sleep while listening to the rain all
    night fill up the Maumee.

I've come a long way to park my car on a nameless street.
I've asked the mirror over and again to erase me from my
    human need.

All of us have written, it seems—at one time or another—a
    long-abandoned novel.
It begins, *Yes, there was the approaching dark, but I swallowed a
    bee intestine instead.*

I have been praying to Borges to reveal to me the much-
    maligned library of my own madness.
Book after book has come to me, with fluttering pages, as if
    they were the wind in my throat that has written every
    word I failed to read.

George Kalamaras

House Hunting During the Egg-Laying Season of Moths

So, the enemy had left their dead and dying behind them.
In general, the air was clean and free from odors.

Still, there was a persistent slit at the end of everyone's nightly dream.
How could we have managed to have arrived in the past, among embers and smoke?

Apparently the anaconda, having swallowed the body, could not negotiate the head of a spike-horn deer.
Too much of our daily lives was being eaten away. Too much left to rot in the ruins.

We had wondered whether we'd heard ourselves correctly.
I asked whether it was really good that I spent so much of my life reading books.

How could we have managed to have arrived in our future?
Complex gifts of the mouth, Desnos told us, are often simple, if not strange.

Whatever cereal was stored in the hut, there was an overhang for rain.
Clumsiness constituted a danger we knew we could not afford.

Robert Desnos Finds His Sleep Medicines...

So, without us, the palm branches were a welfare of almost total disaster.
Shade trees in rain might grant us partial protection and a purposeful home.

A distant noise might mean mosquitoes. Could be moths trying to expel themselves.
Bats, of course, are never known to wake the sleepers they attack.

Having archived the entire correspondence, I have tried to catch a self-evident wound the depth of rain.
Nothing made sense. The only easy decision was to return to the Garden of Eden.

George Kalamaras

This Is How We Know Poetry Matters

Having entered the Milky Way, we felt the Blue Nile
    surge and subside, as if lapping at the banks of a great
    unknowing.
Sure, the Motherland was full of rabies, yellow fever, even reef
    madness on the coasts.

Sometimes I feel as if I can no longer feel the insides of things.
Then I stand by a floor lamp, turning it on and off precisely
    three and one-third times.

When I rediscovered my grandmother's afghan she had
    crocheted for me when I was eighteen, I wondered how
    fifty years could have fallen into a riverous steam.
I remembered the French and Indian War, how I'd read
    every hatchet swing. Felt the bloodletting, the tanning of
    moccasin hides. And knew the hickory trees of the Ohio
    Valley would one day bend their bark toward me.

I could kill an ultimate position.
Stand straight as if inhabiting all the purpose of the possible.

I began to review the mathematical formula for poetry.
It said something about being sure to consume sixty-four
    ounces of heartache a day.

Okay, I'll admit I wanted it both ways at once.
I wanted to spell *Okay* as both O.K. and as *Brilliant-me-my-
    mouth.*

Robert Desnos Finds His Sleep Medicines...

If you unroll the Muslim weaving and find Kabir inside, consider the heft of the weave.
If you plunder the poems of Hafiz, don't be surprised if you find hailstones the size of table salt, dark places where pepper should be, or a gold tooth left below the pillow to coax an unknown voice to enter you.

This Skin or That

Now we take up the study of copper—*blister* copper to be
 exact.
The sun, slantwise through the throat, is a gift of moon-bit
 leaves.

The time of mouth. A choice of plates.
Wind over my voice. A raking across all things gravelly and
 dead.

And so I came to know the triumph of the trichonympha.
I was a protozoan again that lifetime, living in the intestinal
 tract of a termite, breaking up food particles on which to
 survive.

I was a moneyed collector. Examining stamps from French
 Equatorial Africa. From Ubangi-Shari. Nauseous over the
 atrocities. Trading a millipede for a mite.
I was the sun in his groin each week when he left his
 collection of beetles pinned to a leopard skin and moved
 upon his wife.

What are the chances I might go to Spain and secure the guts
 of an orb-weaving spider along a creek's edge?
What is the opportunity to convert my already-smitten wrists
 to copper so that all I touch might gleam?

Drop upon a blanket the milk of a small Andalusian snake.
Shake loose your soul into a considerable confusion of this
 skin or that.

We Remember the Subject of Love

The sky happens from all continents at once.
We remember the subject of love.

Stretch a flag, exuberantly, across a few minutes of a street.
Later, the momentum of the most tragic poems explodes.

Memories mill in the beginning noise of clocks.
I've had an unrequited crush on a certain woman for three
    incarnations in a row now.

Still silent, you have to push night into my belly.
The object of torment is banished to a storm.

Say knives pierce a second infinitude.
Say Antonin Artaud transgressed even the blotting sounds of
    cruel, spiritual love.

Garbage kissed every corner of my mouth.
My poems—not *me*—stood up like a god.

George Kalamaras

Recalcitrant Owl on Fire in the Humble Boy's Chest

That was the lifetime I spent as an eel hunter among the coral
    and crags of Borneo.
Asphalt had poured me there from the memory beds of
    trucks fashioning our mouths.

Phil said the Zen monastery had black painted walls that the
    practitioner was to face for evening's prayer during the
    morning hours.
I know we've struggled with how to fit a pine tree into our
    spine, but only while we sleep.

If I could choose my name, it would be *Recalcitrant Owl on
    Fire in the Humble Boy's Chest.*
If I were reborn as an animal, I would choose the very brief
    life of a fire ant of Namibia.

Ask me to ask you about all the askings of the world.
I will tell you that questioning our answers is the only way to
    interrogate the certainty of ash?

Honestly, I never intended to live this many lives.
Each time, even as I drew closer, I always seemed to remain
    inside the slow step of the moon's insolent bruise. Too
    dark to eat the sun therein. Too far from the depths of the
    deepening deeps.

I Could Not Quite Speak

You might require a hallucination, a thunder juncture struck
    between this spine and that.
Someone might hand you yourself, a Grecian plate with
    nothing but an indecipherable date. A stray flake of parsley.

Sure, you are always welcome, always getting ahead of your
    symptoms.
You are coughing good health even before you survive.

So, the dazzling migration of speech patterns sweats out
    across the tundra.
You are crouched on a rock, examining tufts of scraped-off
    fur.

It is time to follow the herds of fragility locked upon as the
    self.
We are anxious at the heat of it, feeling calm in the key-turned
    tome of a sob.

When the caravan arrived, I was given three baby camels for
    every word I could not quite speak.
I am a rich man now, lying in the grass among the new shoots
    and expanding herds of all that had eluded me.

House and Universe

There were opiates in my blood.
But they came as Hawk. Owl. Bachelard's *intimate immensity*
and *house and universe.*

I forgot about Neruda, though God love him.
I was the tuberculous phlegm of René Daumal. The saliva
spill of an owl on fire in my chest.

I took up backgammon. Dominoes. Gin rummy without the
booze.
I practiced saying things backwards, just to see if my mirror
would stop scolding me.

Mary Ann thought I might need help.
Even Bootsie pawed the fly dung at my feet.

I became less and less certain of my certainty.
John thought me on the path to self-realization, the way trash
collectors become totemic for how plants and animals
exhale their inhalations, repurposing them into the trees.

But it was months before I realized Julio Cortázar was
rewriting the *Oxford Guide to Grammar* into one of the
three lost languages of salt.
Even before he recast both the Old and New Testaments
as just one of the 251 Hindu Upanishads. As a single
hexagram of the *I Ching*. As *The Secret Life of Plants*
rewritten as *A Treatise on Alternate Nostril Breathing.*

Which meant he was still alive. Somewhere north of *very much*. Of the compassionate grasp of *and well*. Perhaps in the poems of Alvaro Cardona-Hine.
Which meant, Alvaro, too, must be somehow back in Costa Rica, sunbathing, soothingly, with a beached whale while listening to its heartache and trying to heal it.

Honestly, it wasn't as confusing as you might at first think.
Robert Desnos's voice was there, mingling with his sleep medicines, beneath Bachelard's floorboards.

And I knew something great and awful and gifts us was there, as well, beneath each step I'd been hesitant to take.
There, waiting for me to finally look down during the beautifully cruel act of looking up.

Notes

The epigraphs are drawn from: Gaston Bachelard, from *The Poetics of Space*, translated by Maria Jolas, Beacon Press, 1969, and from Robert Desnos, from the poem "Lying Down," from *The Selected Poems of Robert Desnos*, translated by Carolyn Forché and William Kulik, The Ecco Press, 1991.

In "The Psychoanalysis of Fire," this poem title and the passage *At the center are the seeds; at the center is the engendering fire* come from Gaston Bachelard, *The Psychoanalysis of Fire*, translated by Alan C. Ross, Beacon Press, 1964.

In "Mizzle," the line "The Maumee River's path from Fort Wayne, Indiana, to Defiance, Ohio, is so tortuous that settlers estimated the water took 160 miles to travel the 100" is a nearly verbatim passage from *A Guide to Natural Areas of Northern Indiana: 125 Unique Places to Explore*, Steven Higgs, Indiana University Press, 2019.

In "My Vocabulary Did This to Me," the quote *Animals move and plants vegetate, oysters and tumbleweeds notwithstanding* comes from *Strangest Creatures on Earth: Adventures Among Fantastic Living Animals*, N. J. Berrill, edited by Edward M. Weyer Jr., Sheridan House, 1953. The poem title comes from Jack Spicer's final words and from the book title *My Vocabulary Did This to Me: The Collected Poetry of Jack Spicer*, Jack Spicer, edited by Peter Gizzi and Kevin Killian, Wesleyan University Press, 2008.

In "The Long Ride," the passage attributed to Jacques Cousteau, *Breathing under water is an attractive notion*, comes from his book *The Silent World*, Captain J. Y. Cousteau (with Frédéric Dumas), Harper & Brothers Publishers, 1953.

"Zorba the Greek" takes its title from the title of a novel by Nikos Kazantzakis, *Zorba the Greek*, translated by Carl Wildman, Simon and Schuster, Inc., 1952.

In "At the Corner of Vallejo and Wang Wei," the line *In my middle years* . . . comes from a poem by Wang Wei, "My Cottage at Deep South Mountain," translated by Tony Barnstone, Willis Barnstone, and Xu Haixin, *Laughing Lost in the Mountains: Poems of Wang Wei*, University Press of New England, 1991.

In "Borges and the Library of Babel," the line "the curvature of the earth" is drawn from the title of a collaborative book of poetry by Gene Frumkin and Alvaro Cardona-Hine, *The Curvature of the Earth*, University of New Mexico Press, 2007.

In "House Hunting During the Egg-Laying Season of Moths," the line "Bats, of course, are never known to wake the sleepers they attack" is taken from *Mammals of Eastern Asia*, G. H. H. Tate, The Macmillan Company, 1947. The poem's title draws from the line "It was the egg-laying season for moths" from Kawabata Yasunari's novel *Snow Country*, translated by Edward G. Seidensticker, Alfred A. Knopf, Inc., 1957.

"House and Universe" takes its title from the title of Chapter 2 in Bachelard's *The Poetics of Space*, noted above. The number of Upanishads noted in the poem is debatable, as there is some discrepancy regarding the exact number. Traditionally, the number of Upanishads is given as 108. However, this number varies among sources, with at least one counting 251 texts that constitute the body of the Upanishads.

The authorship of other occasional quotations in this book should hopefully be clear from the various contexts in which these quotations appear.

Acknowledgments

I want to thank the editors of the following magazines, where some of these poems, or their previous versions, first appeared:

Anvil Tongue: "The Fifth Manifesto," "In the Time of Borges and Calm," "Michael Mitsakis Thought That Every Six Was a Nine," "We Knew Something Good," and "We Remember the Subject of Love"

The Bitter Oleander: "No One Persecuted a Single Word" and "This Skin or That"

Clade Song: "Jacques Cousteau Was a Splendid Blue Shadow," "My Vocabulary Did This to Me," and "We Might Somehow Save the Waning"

Hamilton Stone Review: "Zorba the Greek"

Midwest Quarterly: "Every Word I Failed to Read" and "Recalcitrant Owl on Fire in the Humble Boy's Chest"

Sulfur Surrealist Jungle: "Fire-Eater," "The Hole," "I Could Not Quite Speak," "Initial Me as You Would," "The Speaking Point," and "This, Our Family"

SurVision: "Borges and the Library of Babel," "Jacques Cousteau and the Dark Lengths of Rain," and "Robert Desnos Finds His Sleep Medicines Beneath Bachelard's Floorboards"

Talisman: "A Brief History of Mirrors," "Dostoevsky's Donkey Ride," "The Meticulous Mice of the Lantern-Lathed Tongue," and "Traveling North"

Taos Journal of Poetry: "After Thirty-Two Years"

Word for/Word: "Anywhere We Step," "Brahms by Firelight," and "There Seemed Nowhere Else to Go"

Great thanks to my wife, Mary Ann Cain, for all we share in work and love. Special thanks to John Bradley for being my best and most devoted reader. My poetry is continuously nourished by the love and attention of several other friends, especially Eric Baus, Michelle Comstock, Ray Gonzalez, Patrick Lawler, John Olson, Paul B. Roth, Geoffrey Rubinstein, Lawrence R. Smith, Tony Trigilio, and Lisa and John Zimmerman. Special thanks to Jim Whitcraft for his discerning eye. In addition, I want to thank my former poetry teachers who have given so much to my work through their teaching and friendship: Don Byrd, Mary Crow, Judith Johnson, Roger Mitchell, Bill Tremblay, and the late Philip Appleman. Who could ask for better compadres on the poetic path than my wife and these friends and teachers? Furthermore, none of these poems would be possible without the yogis of India and the mountain hermits of China—past and present—whose quiet contemplation continuously guides my life. Gaston Bachelard—thank you for shining light on the "intimate immensity" of the cellars, nests, and corners of the psyche. And Robert Desnos—wherever you are—I hope these poems enter the glorious depths of your dream, bring you calm, and nourish the "simple and strange" in "everything" you ever loved.

About the Author

GEORGE KALAMARAS, former Poet Laureate of Indiana (2014–2016), is Professor Emeritus of English at Purdue University Fort Wayne, where he taught for thirty-two years. He is the author of twenty-four collections of poetry—fifteen full-length books and nine chapbooks—as well as a critical study on Western language theory and the Eastern wisdom traditions, *Reclaiming the Tacit Dimension: Symbolic Form in the Rhetoric of Silence* (State University of New York Press, 1994). He is the recipient of numerous grants and awards, including a Creative Writing Fellowship from the National Endowment for the Arts (1993) and two Individual Artist Fellowships from the Indiana Arts Commission (2001 and 2011). During 1994, he spent several months in India on an Indo-U.S. Advanced Research Fellowship. In addition to his publications in the United States, his poems have appeared in print journals in Africa, Asia, Europe, and Latin America and have been translated into Bengali and Spanish. George and his wife, writer Mary Ann Cain, have nurtured beagles in their home for nearly thirty years, first Barney, then Bootsie, and now Blaisie. George, Mary Ann, and Blaisie divide their time between Fort Wayne, Indiana, and Livermore, Colorado, in the mountains north of Fort Collins.

www.ingramcontent.com/pod-product-compliance
Lightning Source LLC
Chambersburg PA
CBHW020358170426
43200CB00005B/215